COLLECTING STAMPS

BY

Stephen Holder

ILLUSTRATED BY

Ron Hayward

AND

Norman Reynolds

MACDONALD

First published 1979

Macdonald Educational Ltd
Holywell House
Worship Street
London EC2A 2EN

©Macdonald Educational 1979
ISBN 0 356 063275 (paperback)
ISBN 0 356 063674 (hardback)

Printed by New Interlitho,
Milan, Italy

About this book

This book has been carefully planned to help you become an expert. Look for the special pages to find the information you need. **RECOGNITION** pages, with a **bright green flash** in the top right-hand corner, contain all the essential information to know and remember. **PROJECT** pages, with a grey border, suggest some interesting ideas for things to do and make. At the end of the book there is a useful **REFERENCE SECTION**.

Collecting stamps

All over the world millions of people are stamp collectors. Some go about it in a small way, but others have great collections on which they spend much time and effort. Kings and queens, the rich and famous, and all kinds of ordinary people have found an interest in these little bits of paper.

Why collect stamps?

It's hard to explain the 'magic ingredient' that makes collecting and studying stamps (philately) so enjoyable. Some people like the excitement of searching for certain kinds of stamps – and, at last, finding them. Others hope to discover a valuable stamp. With stamps, you can become an expert now and still enjoy collecting when you're 60.

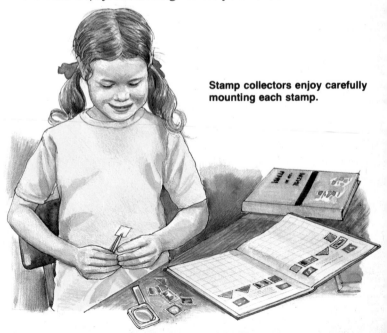

Stamp collectors enjoy carefully mounting each stamp.

**Montenegro,
Prince Nicholas I**

**Antioquia
Coat of arms**

**Great Britain,
Battle of Hastings**

**United States,
Abraham Lincoln**

Learning from stamps

You can learn a lot from stamps. They can make
school subjects come alive. Much of the history of
the world is shown on them – battles, ancient
civilizations and voyages of discovery. Famous men
and women from ancient to modern times – Caesar,
Columbus, Lincoln, Joan of Arc, Shakespeare and
Napoleon – are all on stamps.

Geography is made easy, and the names and
changing patterns of the world are seen. Do you
know where to find Montenegro or Antioquia, Alwar
or Yunnan-Fau? It's easy with stamps to show you.
Kings and coinage, rivers and volcanoes, coats of
arms and flags, important crops and industries – you
will find them all.

A treasure trove

And all the time you're collecting, there's a chance
you might find something valuable. Most stamps are
common, but some are of great value.

Where to begin

Millions of stamps pass through the post each day.

You can begin your collection from the letters that arrive at your home.

Every day, stamps arrive at your home and your school, at offices and banks, shops and hotels. Most are thrown away unwanted, and that is where collecting starts.

First, try to get as many different stamps as you can from your own country. You may be surprised to discover how many there are.

Stamps from abroad

Soon you will want to start collecting stamps from other countries, too. Where do you find them? A few of the letters you receive at home may be from friends or relatives abroad. Perhaps they can send you more stamps from the countries where they live. Your parents may work in offices that deal with foreign places. See if they can bring you stamps from work.

It is quite likely that relations or people you know have collected stamps at some time. They may even have a collection they don't want any more. It is surprising how many people have a few stamps tucked away in a drawer, in case someone would like them. Let other people know you're interested, and stamps will come your way.

Buying stamps

Sooner or later, if you want to extend your collection, you will have to buy some stamps. Many shops have little packets of 25, 50, 100, 500 or 1,000 different stamps which are quite inexpensive. Sorting and examining these will teach you all the basic rules of the game.

Many shops have packets of stamps in rows on windows and doors.

Soaking off and cleaning

Stamps should never be torn straight off the envelope as this will almost always damage the stamp. There are various ways to lift or soak off a stamp. The usual method is with water.

Most stamps are made with colourfast inks that will not 'run' in water. Some old stamps, and those on coloured covers which may shed colour, should be handled separately. The work should be done with great care.

Cutting
First cut neatly round the stamp, leaving a small margin of paper on all sides. Take care not to damage the edges.

Soaking
Place the stamps, face upward, on clean, white, wet blotting paper.

Or, use a bowl of water. The water will slowly soak through the backing paper and loosen the glue.

Cleaning and drying
When you have removed the stamp, rinse it in clean water to take off any glue or dirt. Place it face down to dry on a clean tray or dry blotting paper. The printed face can stick, so move the stamp from time to time.

Lifting
After a while the stamp will gently peel from the paper. Do not be too hasty. Stamps are weaker when wet. First try this with stamps that do not matter.

Pressing
As they dry out, your stamps will probably curl at the edges. To straighten them, they can either be carefully pressed flat under a weight, when quite dry, or placed in the pages of a stock-book, (see page 19).

What to collect?

At first the best idea is to collect everything –
stamps from all countries, old and new. Examine
them, and put together stamps from the same
country. Sort your stamps on a tray or clean table
and slip the separated lots into little envelopes, ready
for when there are more to be added.

You will notice that some stamps have the same
design but different colours and values. Collectors
call these 'sets', and they should be kept together.
Most countries have these definitive sets, with values
for all the postal rates, perhaps changing colour and
value over many years.

A set of 'Sower' designs from France.

**Queen Elizabeth II
'Machin' head, in
use in Britain since
1967.**

Fiji, map of islands, with and without '180°'.

India, statue reversed.

Iceland, King Christian X, with head and background redrawn.

Arranging your stamps

Label your envelopes of sorted stamps and arrange them for easy reference. You can put them in alphabetical order or arrange the countries in groups, by area. You might divide them into Europe, British Commonwealth, America, Africa and Asia. Many stamp albums and catalogues are divided this way. When you start, choose a way you like and understand. You can always change it later.

Swapping stamps

When you are sorting, you will soon find duplicates – two stamps that look the same. Keep them for exchanging with other collectors – or 'swapping'. But be careful – many stamps that look alike are actually different. Sometimes the designs differ very slightly. For example, a small detail may have been left out. Other times the paper, colour, or perforations may vary – as you will soon discover. Look at the stamps at the top of this page. Can you see the differences?

Identifying your stamps

The world has many different languages, and most countries use their own language on their stamps. Often the alphabet is different from ours. One of the first skills you will need is the ability to identify from which country a stamp has come. The 'stamp finder' on page 58 will help you.

OSTERREICH, Austria

Bulgaria

BELGIE or BELGIQUE, Belgium

CESKOSLOVENSKO, Czechoslovakia

DEUTSCHE BUNDESPOST, West Germany

DEUTSCHES REICH, Germany until 1945

SUOMI, Finland

ΕΛΛΑΣ or HELLAS, Greece

ISLAND, Iceland

MAGYARORZAG,
Hungary

NEDERLAND,
The Netherlands

SVERIGE,
Sweden

ESPAÑA,
Spain

ROMANA,
Romania

POLSKA,
Poland

CCCP,
Soviet Union

Arabic numerals

Cyrillic letters.

Б b	**В** v	**Г** g	**Д** d
Е ye	**Ж** zh	**З** z	**И** ee
Л l	**Н** n	**П** p	**Р** r
С s	**У** oo	**Ф** f	**Х** kh
Ц t	**Ч** ch	**Ш** sh	**Щ** sch
Э e	**Ю** yoo	**Я** yah	

HELVETIA,
Switzerland

Japan China Korea

Country symbols used on
stamps.

Different collections

There are two forms of stamps – unused and used.
Unused or 'mint' stamps are as you would buy them
in the post office. A used stamp is one that has been
sent through the mail. Some people collect only one
or the other, but to begin with it is probably best to
collect both.

unused or mint

used in the post

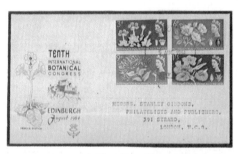

A First Day Cover of the 1964
Botanical Congress issue of
Great Britain on a special envelope.

First Day Covers

In recent years it has become popular to collect new
stamps on First Day Covers. On the day of issue,
collectors buy the new stamps, stick them on
envelopes and post them to themselves. In many
countries the post office offers specially printed
envelopes and a special first-day-of-issue postmark.
There are firms that will arrange the service for you.

Multiples

Many people like to collect stamps that are joined together into pairs, strips or blocks. These are called multiples. Modern issues in blocks of four are especially popular. Stamps are printed in sheets with coded printing details in the margin. Some collectors like to keep these marginal marks attached.

Old stamps are almost always worth far more in any multiple. Pairs, strips and blocks are best kept intact, at least until you have asked for advice.

A corner block of four, showing the printer's markings.

printer's markings

Thematic or topical collections

Some people like to collect stamps on one theme, with designs that show birds, vehicles, sports or other subjects. These are called thematic or topical collections. Stamps are not grouped by the country where they were issued, but by the design. The stamps above would be in a collection of flowers, not Great Britain. For more on thematic collecting, see pages 44–47.

Stamp collecting equipment

Collecting stamps can be done very simply with hardly any equipment at all. But there are a number of aids which will help you. Almost all of them are inexpensive, and most will last for many years. Some are used for studying stamps in detail. Others are for handling and storage.

▲**Tweezers.** Mechanical 'fingers' for handling stamps without getting them dirty or smudged.

▲**Magnifying glass.** Used to examine stamps carefully. Can help you spot flaws or mistakes.

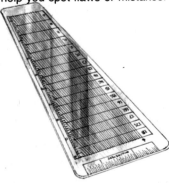

▲**Perforation gauge.** Measures the size of the 'teeth' on the edge of stamps, which vary greatly.

▲**Stamp hinges or mounts.** Small pieces of lightly gummed paper used to mount stamps neatly and safely.

▲Watermark detector. Benzine is dropped from a bottle on to the back of a stamp in a tray. This reveals any watermark, or faint pattern in the paper. Benzine is very flammable so handle carefully.

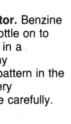

▲Chalk-surface detector. Small stick with a silver tip which leaves a mark on chalk-surface paper. Used occasionally to identify paper.

▲Surcharge measure. An adjustable pair of dividers used to measure overprints, surcharges or inscriptions.

▲Mounting strip. A black gummed paper, with a clear plastic front. Used for mounting mint stamps (or others) without hinges.

▲Johfra sweat-box. A box with a damp pad used to clean hinges or attached paper from mint stamps without damaging glue. Works by condensation.

UV lamp. Uses ultra-violet light to detect phosphor or fluorescent markings, and to check for repaired or forged stamps.

Catalogues and stock-books

A catalogue can be a collector's most useful aid.

Using a catalogue

Since the first stamps appeared in 1840, thousands
of different designs have been issued. To help the
collector, catalogues are available to tell him what
there is to collect and how much it would cost to
buy. The catalogues include illustrations of the
designs, and the stamps are grouped in sets and
arranged in order with the oldest first.

There are many kinds of catalogues. Some cover
the whole world, and others only one country. You
should first become familiar with a simplified
whole-world catalogue. The main ones are those
published by Stanley Gibbons (British), Yvert and
Tellier (French), Michel (German) and Scott (US).

The job of a stock-book

The task of sorting stamps into countries and sets means that you will need a book in which stamps can be moved about as new ones are added or different groups are made. The stock-book was designed to do this job.

How to use it

A stock-book has firm pages with horizontal lines of long, thin pockets, each not as tall as a stamp. The pockets are made from strips of clear plastic fixed at the sides and at the bottom. Stamps can be slipped into them, and easily moved around.

Stock-books are made with few or many pages, bound or loose-leaf. They can be used for all kinds of sorting or storage. Always move stamps carefully in the stock-book, as the perforations can catch on the pockets.

Stamps stored in a stock-book can be easily moved about.

Your stamp album

Once you have collected a number of stamps, you will want to keep them in a stamp album. These have been made for more than a hundred years in many different forms and sizes, for different needs. Start simply with a small bound album with squares printed on the pages.

▼First album
Begin with an inexpensive album like this one. The squares make mounting easier.

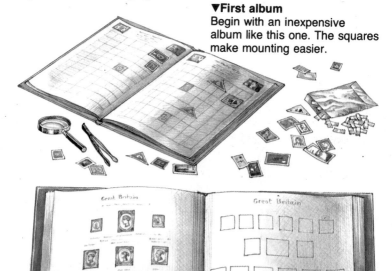

▲Illustrated
Here, pictures and facts are printed on the left.

The page on the right has a space for each stamp.

loose-leaf album

▲Loose-leaf
A spring-back loose-leaf album like this one has movable pages.

The spine of the album has a strong spring which clamps the pages firmly together. You can open the spring and change the order of the pages.

▲Hinged pages
In the best albums, the pages lie flat when the book is open. This makes mounting and study of the stamps much easier.

▲Peg binders
Some loose-leaf binders are made with pegs or posts. Others are made with rings. The pages are easily moved about.

▼Page design
Sheets for loose-leaf albums normally have a printed border and a faint, ruled pattern like graph paper. Some have transparent sheets of paper between the pages to protect the stamps. The better ones have double linen hinges so the pages will lie flat.

▲A linen hinge or fluted paper edge is used to make the pages lie flat.

21

Mounting your stamps

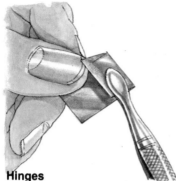

Hinges
Most stamps are mounted with hinges. First fold the hinge about one third of the way down. This gives you a short edge and a large flap. Hinges can be bought folded this way.

Place the stamp face down. Take the hinge and gently moisten the small edge. Fix this part to the back of the stamp, as near to the top as you can, but so that no part of the hinge will show from the front.

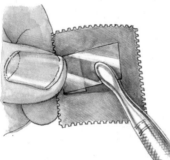

Now moisten the bottom part of the larger flap. Do not wet it too much, and take care not to wet the stamp or it may stick to the page. From the beginning, try to use tweezers for such work. Hands can leave stamps dirty or marked.

Positioning
Position the stamp on the page carefully. Always think first where it is to go. If you make a mistake, leave the stamp to dry for 10 minutes or more. The hinge will then peel off easily.

▲Blocks or strips

Pairs, blocks or strips are fragile at their joining points. It is sometimes better to use a hinge folded on its long side for these. Place the hinge across the perforated joins for support.

▲Triangular stamps

Triangular stamps should be mounted along the edge nearest to the album's spine. This way they will not catch and crease when the page is turned. Attach the hinge along one side.

◄Small and large stamps

For small stamps you can cut hinges in half. For very large or horizontal stamps, fold the hinge on its long side.

►Strip mounts

Many collectors do not like to hinge mint stamps, because they are usually worth more if they have never been hinged. For these stamps (and others if you like) strip mounts can be used. They are made of black backing with a clear plastic front. The stamp is slipped between the two pieces, and the gummed backing stuck to the page. Most strip mounts can be cut to fit the stamp.

◄Mounting covers

First Day Covers and other envelopes are best mounted with corner mounts used for photographs. Choose mounts with clear fronts. Covers mounted in this way can be moved easily.

Presentation

Whether your stamps are common or rare, old or new, it is important that you learn to arrange them properly right from the start. Two album pages are shown below. The stamps on the left-hand page show you what to avoid. They are arranged higgledy-piggledy, are positioned at odd angles and mounted without care. The right-hand page is neat and orderly with room for additions.

Some useful hints
Your pages will look better if older stamps are placed before newer ones, as the styles of design are so different. Sets of stamps and those that are the same size and shape are usually placed together.

Try to avoid messy pages like the one on the left.

Choose a layout that is pleasing to the eye.

Mounting on plain pages

If you are mounting your stamps on a plain page, you have more scope to design your layout. Plan your design before you start mounting. The two pages shown above have been carefully planned and the collector has thought about the number and size of the stamps in each group. The eye likes well-balanced pages like these.

Experiment first

There are always several possible ways to arrange the same set of stamps. Experiment first to see which looks best. You may want to leave room for missing stamps. Never crowd a page. It looks better to have too few stamps than too many.

Sets of stamps with low values are usually placed on the page first, with higher values at the end. But when sets contain several different shapes, you may have to change this order.

Lettering your album

You can buy ready-made page headings on gummed paper – or make your own. Cut out ready-made headings carefully.

Centre the heading on the page, leaving a small margin at the top. Avoid fancy lettering. It is the stamps you are displaying.

You can also use a stencil kit, with the shapes of letters cut out of a piece of plastic.

Choose the letter, position it and trace the shape. Use a pen that will not smudge. A pen called a rapidograph is best.

▲You will need an accurate ruler with measurements in inches and centimetres.

▲To letter without a stencil, use black drawing ink.

▲Position the wording lightly in pencil before inking it.

▲Use a penholder that will allow you to change nibs.

▲Use a soft eraser to remove pencil lines.

▲Nibs are made for different thicknesses and styles.

ABCDEFGHIJKLMN OPQRSTUVWXYZ 1234567890 abcdefghijklmnopq rstuvwxyz

▲Practice this simple, clear alphabet before you begin to letter your pages.

For further advice on lettering, ask an artshop – or a friend who is an artist.

A swap book and stamp map

Early in your collecting life you will come across duplicates, known as 'swaps'. Keep them to exchange with other collectors.

Make a swap book in which to mount your duplicates. Use an old album or stock-book, or a ring binder and plain paper.

What better way to decorate the front than with stamps. But make sure you use only worthless or damaged ones!

You could make a pattern by arranging stamps according to colour. Plan your design carefully before you begin.

Stamp collages are not new. In Britain, the Victorians papered screens, lamp shades and even whole rooms with stamps – some of which would now be worth a fortune if they were not glued down.

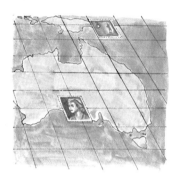

An interesting way to use stamps is to make a stamp map. Posters have been published for this purpose, but it is easy to make your own. Perhaps you can do this as a project at school.

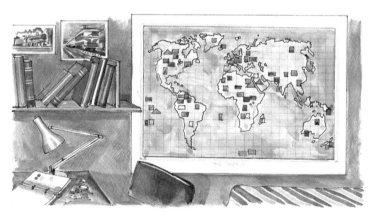

Buy or draw a map of the world. Sort through some stamps, perhaps your swaps, for stamps from various countries.

Mount the stamps in position on the map. Add more as your collection grows. The result can be quite spectacular!

The parts of a stamp

Stamp collecting has its own vocabulary and special terms. A short glossary listing these can be found on page 60. The parts of a stamp and the design are described by special terms. The enlarged pictures of two French stamps below show some of these. Try to identify the parts of some of your stamps.

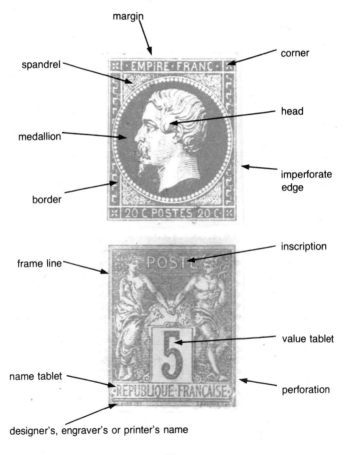

margin

corner

spandrel

head

medallion

imperforate edge

border

inscription

frame line

value tablet

name tablet

perforation

designer's, engraver's or printer's name

Perforation

Perforation is the way two or more stamps are separated. The first stamps were imperforate. Then forms of paper cuts (roulettes) were tried, followed by punched holes.

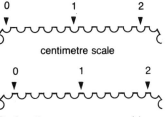

centimetre scale

Perforations are measured by the number of teeth, or holes found in two centimetres.

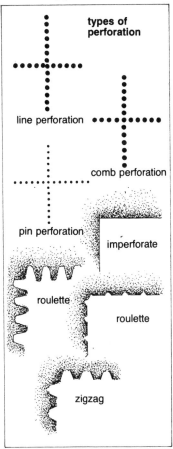

types of perforation

line perforation

comb perforation

pin perforation

imperforate

roulette

roulette

zigzag

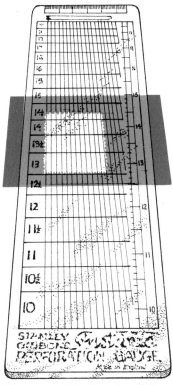

If a stamp has 13½ teeth in two centimetres along the top and 14 on the side, we write: perf. 13½ × 14. The number varies from around 7 to 18.

Measure perforations by sliding a perforation gauge over a stamp until the converging lines match up with the teeth. Then read the number at the side.

Paper and watermarks

The paper used for stamps has varied. The earliest papers were handmade, but now machines make the vast quantities needed. The two main types of stamp paper are 'wove', where the fibres have a smooth finish, and 'laid', where the texture lies in parallel lines. Stamp paper can be thin and almost transparent (**pelure**) or very thick (**carton**).

Special papers
To make it hard to forge stamps, the paper is often treated in some way. **Quadrille** paper has faint squares; **granite** has coloured, hairy fibres. Sometimes one or both sides are coloured. **Chalk-surface** paper has a smooth, shiny finish. In times of war, emergency paper supplies have been used, including old war maps and money.

quadrille

coloured paper

on war map

laid paper   on money

varnished   granite paper

32

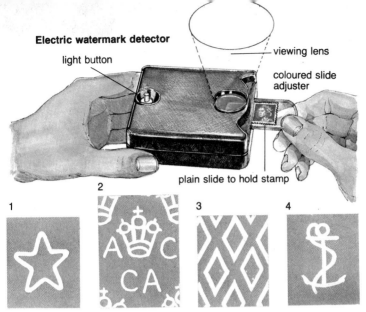

Electric watermark detector

light button

viewing lens

coloured slide adjuster

plain slide to hold stamp

1. India 'star', 2. British Colonial 'multiple crown CA', 3. Germany 'lozenge', 4. Cape of Good Hope 'cabled anchor'.

How watermarks are made

Stamp paper often has a watermark, again to prevent forgeries. This is a pattern pressed into the paper during manufacture. When the paper pulp is still wet, it is passed under a roller fitted with pieces of metal. This thins the paper and makes a design that can be seen when the paper is held against the light.

Watermark detectors

Many watermarks are hard to see. There are two aids to 'reading' them. Place a stamp face down on a black watermark tray, apply a drop of benzine, and the watermark usually appears. The electric watermark detector is a box with a battery and light, with coloured slides to insert above the stamp. The coloured slides blot out the design and should reveal the watermark – although a few are hard to see.

How a stamp is designed and printed

Someone has to design every stamp, and it is not as easy as it may seem. Some primitive stamp designs have been scratched on a flat stone (New Caledonia), typed on a typewriter (Uganda) and engraved on wood (US Civil War issues), but most are carefully prepared by an artist before production. Though the finished stamp is small, the designer does the original artwork on a much larger scale.

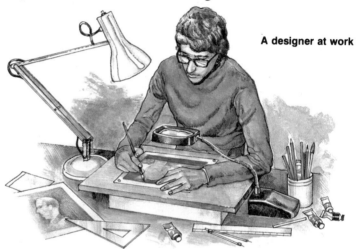

A designer at work

Preparing the artwork
Much research goes into the preparation of the artwork. The designer may use photographs and models to make sure his drawing is accurate. He will often have to work within strict rules as to the wording of the inscription or the size of the value tablet. After the design is approved, it will be engraved in negative on a master die, unless a modern photographic process is being used.

Modern printing

Hundreds of millions of stamps are now needed every day around the world. Specialist firms provide these carefully printed pieces of paper. The quality is strictly checked and the standard has to be high. A great deal of the equipment is electronically controlled, printing perhaps nine colours at once. These machines would astound the early printers.

Large modern printing presses

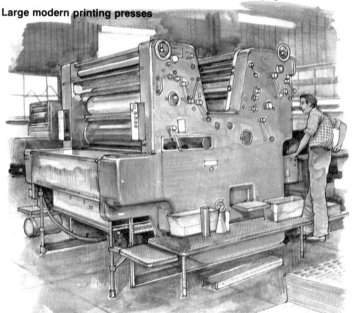

Printing the earliest stamps

In the first days of stamp production, printing machines were much simpler than the giant modern ones, but the quality of the workmanship was high. Many classic stamps are recognized as finely engraved works of art. Fine prints of millions of stamps were produced, but some mistakes were made. Today these rare stamps with errors are eagerly sought and can be quite valuable.

Stamp printing

Stamps are printed by four main methods: **line engraved** or **recess** printing, **typography** (letterpress or surface printing), **lithography** and **photogravure.** A fifth process, **embossing,** is in some respects a mixture of the first two. The methods are complex, but the principles are simple.

Recess printing or line engraving
The design is cut into the metal, and the ink lies in the recessed grooves of the engraving.

Ink in grooves.

'N' is recessed.

Typography or letterpress
The design is raised from the metal, with the ink lying on the raised parts.

Ink on raised parts.

'N' is raised.

Lithography
The design is drawn on treated flat stones or plates. The ink lies only on the design.

Ink on design only.

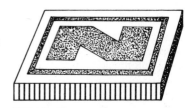

'N' is level.

Embossing
The part of the design on one die is raised and the part on another is flat or recessed.

When paper is pressed between the two, the embossed part stands out from the rest of the design.

Photogravure

This is a more recent process for stamp production, first used in Bavaria in 1914. A design is photographically reproduced on glass or film. A print from this is pressed onto a copper plate.

Acid is used to etch the design in the copper, cutting deeper into the shaded parts. Rotary photogravure (heliogravure) is mass production from curved plates on cylinders of rotary presses.

blue (cyan)

magenta

yellow, magenta and cyan

yellow

yellow and cyan

black

Modern stamp designs are printed from four plates, one for each basic colour (yellow, magenta and cyan) and one black. The paper passes each plate and is printed one colour at a time. To get the final multi-coloured effect, the colours are overlaid and lined up exactly, in perfect 'register'.

completed design

Choosing your speciality

It is good to collect everything at first, but so many stamps have been issued that it is quite impossible for any one person to collect them all. Sooner or later your interest may turn more to one group, country, issue or design, which you can collect and study in more depth.

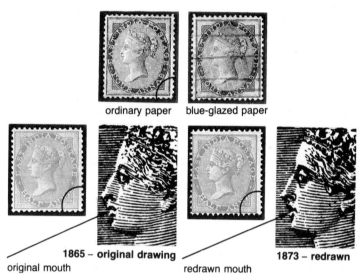

ordinary paper   blue-glazed paper

1865 – **original drawing**   1873 – **redrawn**

original mouth   redrawn mouth

Stamp variations
There is plenty of scope for specialization in the stamps of a single country. The same stamp may appear in a number of shades, or be printed on different papers. There may be small variations in the image, or the design may be slightly redrawn. A different printer may print it, perhaps from new plates. Variations in stamps from India are shown above and on the opposite page.

Other changes to look for

When the post office chooses a different printer, or changes its policies, the final printed stamps may also change. Watermarks change or are introduced where there were none before. Inscriptions may be slightly different, or the printing ink altered. Certain values may change colour as postal rates change. All these variations can be collected mint, used, in blocks or on letters. Then there are the many postal markings to be studied, on single stamps or covers.

No watermark in 1860, with
'Elephants head' watermark in 1865.   1911 pale grey   1922 slate blue

old inscription   new inscription

1902 'India postage'.   1906 inscription redrawn.

Specializing further

The true specialist can then go beyond this to collect the materials used to produce stamps. Artwork, colour trials, proofs, 'specimen' stamps, and postal notices are all of interest. So are printing errors, reprints and forgeries. This leads to the study of postmarks and postal history before the issue of postage stamps.

The first stamps

The world's first stamps were the Penny Black and
Twopenny Blue of Great Britain, issued on 6 May
1840. Switzerland was the second country to issue
stamps. Other countries soon followed. The 12
earliest stamps are shown below. All are now quite
valuable.

**Great Britain, Twopenny Blue,
May 6th 1840, unused**

**Great Britain, Penny Black,
May 6th 1840, used**

**Great Britain, Penny Black, May
6th 1840, unused**

**Great Britain, Twopenny Blue,
May 6th 1840, used**

**Switzerland, canton of Zurich,
March 1843**

**Switzerland, 'Double Geneva',
October 1843**

Brazil, 'Bull's Eye', August 1843

Switzerland, 'Bâle Dove', July 1845

USA, general issues, July 1847

Trinidad, 'Lady McLeod', April 1847

USA, local issues, 1845–46

Mauritius, 'Post Office', September 1847

Bermuda, 'Postmaster', 1848

France, January 1849

Rare and famous stamps

The rarest stamp in the world is shown below. It was found by a schoolboy in British Guiana in 1873 and has since passed through the hands of several collectors. In 1970 it was sold to an American group.

British Guiana, 1 cent black on magenta, 1856 (enlarged)

If the stamps on these two pages were sold, they would probably fetch in excess of **£1 million.**

British Guiana, 'Ship' 1 cent black on magenta, 1852

British Guiana, Cottonreel, 1850–51, on part of a wrapper

Mauritius, 1 penny 'Post Office', 1847, used on cover

Great Britain, VR penny black, 1840, prepared for use but not issued

Canada, twelve pence black, 1851

Canada, pair of ten pence 'Cartier', 1855

Cape of Good Hope Woodblock, 1 penny error of colour, in pair with normal four penny

Cape of Good Hope Triangular, 1 shilling green, 1855

Great Britain, Board of Education official overprint, 1902

Hawaiian 'Missionary', 1851

Moldavia, 'Bull's Head', 1858

Thematic or topical collecting

Some 50 years ago the idea first arose of collecting not by country, but by subject. In Europe these collections are called **thematics,** in the USA, **topicals.** The design on the stamp is the important factor, not the date of issue or place of origin. This can be an entertaining and inexpensive way of collecting. Large collections can easily be made of general subjects such as animals, birds, flowers, sport, space, music, heraldry or writers.

Unfortunately, many countries produce stamps solely to supply this market. Often there is little real need for the stamps. Partly because of this, and partly because some collectors think the idea is 'not serious', the popularity of thematic collections varies.

A collection on space.

Stamps with sports themes.

Special thematic collections

Some people collect the stamps that each country has produced for a special reason. Collections can be made of postage due stamps, military stamps, or issues produced to mark or commemorate events – such as the Olympic Games or World Cup. These collections can be enlarged by adding stamps illustrating the theme. To a collection of military stamps, you could add stamps showing soldiers, medals, weapons and battles. To one of postage due stamps, you could add those showing postmen, post offices and letter boxes.

You can add to your thematic collection, stamps in which the postmark matches the theme. For instance, a stamp postmarked 'Barking' would fit in a collection of stamps on dogs, or animals. A stamp marked in a town where a famous battle took place would go well in a military collection.

Arranging your thematic collection

Once you have chosen a subject, it can be broken down into smaller areas. Your album can be arranged accordingly. A collection of animals could be divided into cats, dogs, horses, and so on. More difficult subjects can be attempted, such as astrology, poetry, medicine, chess – almost anything.

Finding the right stamps

Start looking through stamps with an eye for the design. Packets can be bought on the main themes. The more particular ones will need careful research and can make fine projects. Many books have been published listing stamps by topics, but it is more fun to develop the theme with your own ideas.

Flower stamps from around the world.

Two popular themes are birds (above) and animals (below).

Postal history

Many collectors have taken up the study of postal history – the story of mail from the earliest times to the present day.

This can include collecting and studying all papers, postal markings and forms of mail, some several hundred years older than the first postage stamps. Postal rates are studied, and the way mail was transported; so are stamps, postmarks and the postal equipment used. Postmarks and stamps make up only a small part of the story.

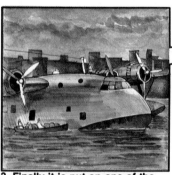

3. Finally it is put on one of the early trans-Atlantic mail flights to New York.

2. From there, a vehicle takes it to Bombay, the nearest port. A ship takes it from Bombay to Marseille, in France. Then it goes by train to Paris.

Looking at covers

A simple cover, like an envelope, can tell us many interesting things. A close look at its franking (stamps), cancellation (postmark), transit marks and instructional marks can reveal a wealth of historical detail. What may appear a simple stamp from an ordinary place may prove to be quite the opposite.

One letter's journey

The journey of an imaginary letter from India to New York in about 1930 is shown below. There are many books on postal history that will help you find out how letters travelled between distant places at other times in the past.

1. A runner takes the letter from a remote village to a nearby town.

A postal study of your area

▲A map
Start your study by making a map of your area, showing cities, towns, roads, railways and airports.

▲Early transport
Try to find out how the post was carried in the past.

Your local library will be the best place to start.

▲Look for letters from earlier times. Items two hundred years old are quite common and can still be found. Try and discover how the mails were moved from town to town.

▲Sea mail
Mail that arrived by sea may have markings of special interest to collectors.

◀Postcards of your area
Millions of picture postcards were printed. Book and antique dealers have boxes of them to look through. Old picture postcards of your area are still easy to collect and are inexpensive.

▶Early airmail flights
The growth of airmail delivery brought many special hand stamps to record the first flights. There may be some that have a connection with your area.

▲Postal equipment
Don't forget the machinery and equipment of the post, old and new. Post boxes can be particularly interesting and attractive. Try to find out how they've changed in your area over the years.
◀Photographs or drawings of post offices, postmen, post vehicles, old and new, are all part of the story of the post. Take some photographs in your area.

Errors and varieties

Stamps are not always what they seem. Many stamps have errors and some were printed in more than one variety. Some of these are quite rare.

There can be varieties in design, colour, printing, watermark or perforation and there can be errors in all of these. Sometimes a design is wrongly drawn, a watermark missing, a stamp printed in the wrong colour, or a part printed upside down. These varieties add to the interest of your collection.

correct – 'de la methode'

wrong – 'sur la methode'

centre with colour shift

design with normal centre

centre sideways

reversed and imperforate

correctly printed

Overprints and surcharges

Many stamps have had their original purpose or form changed (see below). Stamps may be required for special purposes and currencies may change and require new values.

These changes are made by overprints and surcharges. An overprint is any printed addition to a stamp; surcharges are additions that change its value.

government official military occupation   war tax   different territory

parcel post

airmail

state service

Changes of the original face value of the stamp.

Cancellations

Cancellations were first used to prevent stamps being re-used in the post. Later cancellations show the place, date and time of posting, the postal routing and type of mail. First came the 'Maltese Cross', used to cancel Penny Blacks.

The first cancellation was the 'Maltese Cross', shown above. The earlier named circular date stamp postmarks were used to cancel stamps, and they are still used today.

Numeral 'killers', like those below, showed the number of the office of origin. These three come from Britain, France and Baden.

Some countries used other shapes, like the Spanish 'spider' cancel above.

Germany used the 'horseshoe' and 'box' cancels. What information do they give?

▼Stamps have been cancelled with pen and ink, by hand, when no other means was available.

▼In times of trouble, home-made cancellations (like those of the US Civil War) appeared.

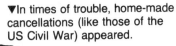

Pen and ink marks

US 'fancy cancels'

▼Special purpose cancellations were created for many different uses.

These include military, airmail, maritime, and railway transmission. A few are shown below.

MILITARY

Bavarian 'feldpost'

Great Britain 'FPO'

French 'poste aux armées'

MARITIME

Many countries 'sea mail'

French 'anchor'

British 'ship letter'

RAILWAY

German 'bahnpost'

German 'zug' (train)

British 'sorting carriage'

Today the pictorial slogan postmark, or 'flamme', is used.

It combines a circular date stamp with a picture and words.

Forgeries, fakes and reprints

In stamp collecting, fakes are stamps that have been improved or altered; forgeries are manufactured copies.

Many forgeries have been made to deceive the stamp collector, but forgeries to deceive the post office are rarer. These are worth much more than the common stamps they copied. The most famous is the British 'Stock Exchange' forgery, produced by a clerk, sold at the stock exchange and not discovered for 25 years.

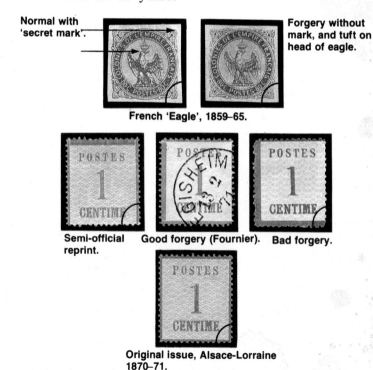

Normal with 'secret mark'.

Forgery without mark, and tuft on head of eagle.

French 'Eagle', 1859–65.

Semi-official reprint.

Good forgery (Fournier).

Bad forgery.

Original issue, Alsace-Lorraine 1870–71.

Original Stamp, Heligoland 1867.   Semi-official reprint.   Forgery (Fournier).

Original stamp, France 'Bordeaux' issue, 1870.   Sperati reproduction.

Great Britain 1 shilling green, 1867–73   'Stock exchange' forgery.

There have been many forgers, some whose work is so bad any collector will soon recognize it. Others have created copies that can be considered works of art, and have become quite well-known: Jean de Sperati worked in France between 1908 and 1953, and was the finest craftsman. François Fournier, a Swiss manufacturer, from 1890 to 1914, made the most facsimilies. The Spiro brothers of Hamburg made their copies during the 1860s and 1870s.

There have also been many others. Samuel Allen Taylor was a member of the 'Boston gang' and George Kirke Jeffryes belonged to the 'London gang'. Above are some original stamps and forgeries.

Reference section

A stamp finder

At first you may find identifying stamps very puzzling. There are many countries however whose names are very like the English or French ones so you will find these easier to recognize. Other identification will become easier with experience. Some of the words you are most likely to come across are listed below. A fuller list is given in the 'XLCR Stamp Finder'.

A PAYER TE BETELEN: Belgium

A PERCEVOIR: Belgium, France, French Colonies, Egypt

A.&T: Annam & Tonkin.

AVISPORTO: Denmark

BAYER, BAYERN: Bavaria

B.C.A: British Central Africa

BENADIR: Italian Somaliland

B.M.A: British Military Occupations (various)

BOGACHES, BOGCHAH: Yemen

C.C.C.P: Russia

C.CH: (on French Colonies) Cochin-China

CESKOSLOVENSKO: Czeckoslovakia

CORREIO(S): Portugal

CORREOS: Spain & Colonies

CPbNJA: Serbia

DANSK-VESTINDISKE, VESTINDIEN: Danish West Indies

DEUTSCH(E), DEUTSCHES REICH: Germany, German group

DIENSTMARKE: Germany & states, Danzig, Saar

DILIGENCIA: Uruguay

DOPLATA: Poland, Central Lithuania

DOPLATIT: Czechoslovakia

DRZAVA, DRZAVNA: Yugoslavia

EESTI: Estonia

EIRE: Ireland, Irish Free State

ESCUELAS: Venezuela

ESPAÑA: Spain

ΕΛΛΑC, ΕΛΛΑΣ ΕΛΛΗΝΙΚΗ: Greece

FRANCO: Spain, Philippines

FRANCOBOLLO: Italy & states

FREIMARKE: German states

FRIMARKE: Denmark, Norway, Sweden

G. (on Cape of Good Hope): Griqualand West

G.E.A: German East Africa Tanganyika

G.P.E., G & D:
Guadeloupe
GUERCHES: Abyssinia
(Ethiopia), Saudi
Arabia
HELVETIA: Switzerland
HRVATSKA: Yugoslavia,
Croatia
ПAPA,ПAPE:
Montenegro, Serbia
INSTRUCCION:
Venezuela
ISLAND: Iceland
JYГOCΠABNJA:
Yugoslavia
K.G.L. POST: Denmark
KLAIPEDA: Memel
KPHTH: Crete
KR, KREUZER: Austria,
Hungary, German
states
LATVIJA, LATWIJA:
Latvia
LIETUVA: Lithuania
MAGYAR,
MAGYARPOSTA,
MAGYARORSZAG:
Hungary
MAPKA: Russia, Finland,
Serbia
MARKA: Estonia
M.E.F: British occupation
of Italian colonies
MQE: Martinique
N.C.E: New Caledonia
NEDERLAND:
Netherlands
NORDDEUTSCHER
POSTBEZIRK: N.
German Confederation
NORGE: Norway
N.S.B: Nossi-Be
N.S.W: New South Wales

OFFENTLIG SAK:
Norway
OSTERREICH: Austria
PACCHI POSTALI: Italy,
San Marino
PARA: Egypt, Turkey,
foreign offices in Turkey
PCCP: Russia
PEN, PENNI: Finland
PIASTER, PIASTRE:
Foreign offices in Turkey
POCZTA, POLSKA:
Poland
PORTO: Austria
PREUSSEN: Prussia
QUINTAR, QUINDAR:
Albania
REICH, REICHPOST:
Germany
REIS: Portugal
R.S.A: South Africa
SAARGEBIET: Saar
SACHSEN: Saxony
SEGNATASSE: Italy
SHQIPENIE, SHQIP-
TARE: Albania
SLOVENSKO: Slovakia
SOLDI: Austrian Italy
S.P.M: St. Pierre &
Miquelon
SUIDAFRIKA: South
Africa
SUOMI: Finland
SVERIGE: Sweden
TE BETALEN:
Netherlands & Colonies,
Belgium
T.E.O: French Syria, Cilicia
ULTRAMAR: Spanish
Colonies
VAN DIEMEN'S LAND:
Tasmania
YCTAB: Montenegro

Glossary

Adhesive: a gummed postage stamp as opposed to one printed on a card or envelope.

Approvals: a dealer's priced selection sent by post.

Bisect: a stamp cut in half used officially due to a shortage of stamps.

Block: 4 or more stamps joined together, other than in a strip.

Cachet: a descriptive hand stamp on an envelope, usually for a special event.

Cancellation: a mark struck on a stamp to show it has been used.

Coil: a roll of stamps for use in stamp machines.

Colour trial: test printing of a stamp for selection of colour.

Commemorative: stamp issued to commemorate a person or event.

Cover: an envelope or wrapper complete with postmarks and/or stamps.

C.T.O: cancelled to order. Stamps not used but cancelled before sale to dealers or collectors.

Definitives: stamps produced for everyday use as opposed to Commemoratives or special issues.

Die: the original engraved design from which the printing plates are made.

Error: a stamp issued with accidental but marked differences from the normal (see Variety).

Essay: design printed for consideration but not issued.

Face Value: the monetary value shown on the stamp.

Fake: a genuine stamp or cover that has been altered to seem better than it is or repaired.

F.D.C: first day cover; stamps on a cover postmarked the day of issue.

Fiscals: stamps printed or used for revenue purposes.

Forgery: an imitation of a stamp, overprint or postmark.

Imperf(orate): without perforations, as in most early issues.

Laid paper: paper with a texture of lines, horizontal or vertical.

Locals: stamps produced and valid for only local use.

Margins: the plain surrounds of a stamp design, especially imperfs; the borders of a complete sheet.

Mint: an unused stamp in perfect condition, with undisturbed gum.

Multiple: a group of 3 or more unseparated stamps.

Obliteration: Any mark used to cancel a stamp.

Official: stamp produced for use by a government department.

Overprint: an inscription or device additionally printed on to a stamp.

Pane: a division of a sheet of stamps; a page of a stamp booklet.

Pelure: A thin hard paper; often used to describe any very thin paper.

Phospher lines: colourless lines printed on stamps, needed for automatic letter-sorting equipment.

Plate numbers: numbers identifying printing plates, sometimes printed in the stamp design.

Postage due: labels used by the Post Office to indicate unpaid mail charges.

Pre-adhesive: a letter or cover used before the introduction of adhesive stamps.

Pre-cancel: stamps sold already postmarked for use on bulk mail.

Proof: a trial print to check the design is correct before printing for use.

Regionals: stamps prepared for use in one area of a country (G.B.).

Remainders: stamps remaining when an issue is withdrawn from use, usually destroyed but sometimes sold to collectors, often with C.T.O. cancellation.

Reprint or **Reimpression:** printings made (officially or privately) from original plates at a later date.

Retouch: an alteration cut by an engraver into a plate to correct an error or damage.

Roulette: a form of perforation where paper is punctured by pins or blades but no paper is removed.

Se tenant: two different stamps that are joined together.

Spandrel: the triangular space between a curved centre and the rectangular frame around it.

Specimen: a stamp so overprinted by the post office. Used for illustrative purposes only and not postally valid.

Strip: 3 or more stamps joined together in a line.

Surcharge: an overprint which changes the face value of a stamp.

Tête-bêche: two stamps joined together, one upside down.

Variety: a small difference from normal in a design, as opposed to an error.

Watermark: a design impressed into paper during production for security reasons.

Wove paper: paper with a plain even texture, much like cloth.

Finding out more

Books

The literature of philately is enormous – perhaps more than in any other hobby. It is difficult to single out books from so many, but useful guides to general collecting are:

Teach yourself Stamp Collecting by L. N. and M. Williams (Knight Books)

Postage Stamps in the Making by J. Easton (Faber and Faber)

The Postage Stamp by L. N. and M. Williams (Penguin).

How to Arrange and Write Up a Stamp Collection by Stanley Philipps and C. P. Rang (Gibbons)

Fundamentals of Philately by L. N. and M. Williams (Heinemann)

Magazines

These are the main general magazines in the UK: *Stamp Collecting Weekly; Philatelic Magazine* (monthly); *Stamp Magazine* (monthly); *Gibbons Stamp Monthly.*

Clubs and societies

There are lots of these – from local clubs to large societies with international memberships.

Find out the address of your local club from your library, or write to:
The British Philatelic Foundation
1 Whitehall Place
London SW1A 2HE.

This is also the address of the **National Philatelic Society,** which is the largest in Britain.

The premier society in the world is:
The Royal Philatelic Society
41 Devonshire Place
London W1N 1PE.

Stamp dealers

The most famous dealers in the world, now a vast organization, are:
Stanley Gibbons Ltd
391 Strand
London WC2R 0LX.

There are many other fine firms – including the famous auction houses:
Robson Lowe Ltd
50 Pall Mall
London SW1Y 5JZ.

Harmers of London
41 New Bond Street
London W1A 4EH.

Index

Acknowledgements

The following illustrations are reproduced by gracious permission of Her Majesty the Queen: Mauritius 'Post Office', September 1847 (page 41); Cape of Good Hope Woodblock, triangular pair (page 43).

Other illustrations of rare and famous stamps are reproduced by kind permission of Stanley Gibbons Ltd., Robson Lowe Ltd., the Royal Philatelic Society, London, and J. H. Levett R.D.P., F.R.P.S.L. The author and publishers acknowledge grateful thanks to them all.

Special thanks are due to
Norman Reynolds for all his
help in the preparation and
design of this book.